EVERYTHING WE SHOULD HAVE TAUGHT YOU

IN HIGH SCHOOL, BUT NEVER DID

The Graduation Gift of Life's Most Important Lessons

Dr. Richard Gary Shear

Published by The Shear Advantage Inc.

Copyright 2023 by Richard Gary Shear

Edited by Patricia B. Molloy

Cover design by Jeffrey Andersen

ISBN: 979-8-9879449-0-5

Introduction

Schools Did Not Teach Us What We Needed to Know

Wouldn't it be great if in high school we were taught the tips for a better life? High school taught us how to determine the area of a room, but not how to deal with the people we find in that room. High school taught us the cataclysmic events of history, but rarely touched on the life struggles we were currently experiencing and later would experience. Life can be and is better when we learn life's most important lessons.

In high school, we were taught math, social studies, science, English, world languages, physical education, and more. What wasn't taught were the important tips that will help make your life a success. We desire a life with incredible goodness, wonderful moments, bliss, meaningfulness, great relationships, and joy. We want to avoid bad choices and poor decisions. Even though we want help in navigating life; high schools were not designed to provide it.

For many years as a principal, I led the graduates of four separate high schools through their educational life to their graduation ceremony. Aware of the important matters left untaught, I converted the graduation address to *Everything We Should Have Taught You in High School, But Never Did. The Graduation Gift of Life's Most Important Lessons.*

This book comprises the understandings I shared with my graduates designed to make their lives better, easier, more successful, more peaceful, and more joyful. I hope and believe it will help you as well.

There Are Two Secrets to Success

The Ability to Get Up When Knocked Down

The Ability to Connect With Others Through Effective Communication

If there is one question many high school students think about on graduation day, it is, what do I need to do to be successful? The best way to answer that question is to look at successful people and see what they have in common. While there are many variables which lead to success, successful people share two main characteristics: they persevere and possess well-developed communication skills. Perseverance is the ability to keep going forward even when knocked down. Walt Disney, Abraham Lincoln, and Thomas Edison had a string of defeats in life. What they had in common was the ability to move forward in the face of defeat and to communicate effectively with others. Often, the difference between successful people and unsuccessful people is that successful people get up, dust themselves off, and try again.

The door to success may not open easily, so be flexible and willing to create a new plan. Get a hammer, nails, some wood, and build yourself a new door. Work the problem and don't give up. The ability to communicate and be resilient will enhance your chances for success. If you work on those two skills, success is a much more likely outcome.

Remember, the resilient are brilliant.

Forgiveness Is Not a Gift You Give to Others

It Is a Gift You Give to Yourself

Famed comedian Groucho Marx was asked when he was in his 80s, what is the key to a long life? Groucho replied "have a lot of friends." The follow-up question was, how do you go about having a lot of friends? Groucho replied "have a short memory." Comedians have a unique insight into how people think. Their art form is built on understanding human expectations and tinkering with them. Groucho understood people will disappoint you. Loved ones will disappoint, relatives will disappoint, best friends, acquaintances all disappoint.

One of the keys to a long life and happiness is to learn to forgive the people who have let you down. People make mistakes, they do dumb things, they believe dumb things – forgive them. People can be selfish, inconsiderate, rude, weak – forgive them. There is a secret reward to forgiveness; it is not a gift you are granting to another; it is a gift you are giving to yourself. A lack of forgiveness is always accompanied by harsh judgment, anger, and bad feelings. These bad feelings rot away the container from the inside out. The container that is rotting away is you. Just as sulfuric acid corrodes the inside of a metal container, not forgiving, will corrode you.

Here is the first major lesson we should have taught you in high school: forgive others who have hurt you because it is good for you. Forgiving them doesn't mean you forgot what they did to you. Forgiving them doesn't mean you have accepted what they did as less painful. It means that you are no longer granting them space in your head to hurt you. It means you have too many good things to think about to focus on bad thoughts.

Forgiving others is actually a gift you give yourself.

To Have a Successful Life

You Have to Be Kind to You

We make decisions based on the information we have at the time. Yet, we are quite talented at making ourselves miserable for making a choice we now regret. We can extend bad feelings to a day, a week, a year, and even a lifetime. During the course of our lives, there are many choices we regret. There is no one walking the earth who would not do something differently if given the chance to go back in time. As important as it is to forgive others to have a happy life, it is more important to forgive ourselves. Whatever the cause and the thought process that brought you to regret; practice forgiving you. The time we spend on earth will pass quickly; do not waste it being angry at yourself for not being perfect.

The condition of perfection is fictitious; it does not exist in reality. You have a choice about past regrets. You can forgive yourself or live with regret. However, there are few things that are more important to a successful life than learning from mistakes and moving past them. One is, do not dwell on the things you should have done better. Instead, learn from past mistakes to avoid repeating them. Once you recognize mistakes are part of life, you will be better equipped to learn from them. You will learn that living with regret for mistakes is just a foolish and hurtful waste of time. Always remember, we make the best decisions we can with the information we have at the time. Embrace self-forgiveness.

Self-forgiveness is liberating!

We Weren't Designed to Walk Backward for a Good Reason

It Would Slow Us Down and We'd Bump into Things

Self-forgiveness must be accompanied by thinking differently. To live each day thinking of pain from the past is a tragic mistake. In life, we can't walk forward while looking back. We all want to fix the mistakes we have made on our journey through life. That is true for the 17-year-old and the 70-year-old. We have all made the wrong choices, were in the wrong place at the wrong time, and passed on great opportunities. We have all trusted the wrong person at times in our life.

Those situations are called "life experiences." Mother Theresa put it this way: Yesterday is gone. Tomorrow has not yet come. We have only today.

We rarely if ever look back on all the right decisions we have made. However, we are much better off using our time to celebrate our good decisions. The only reason to revisit a bad decision is to learn from it. Begin each day optimistic about the joy today will bring and the many opportunities for success to come. Look forward and walk excitedly into your today. After all, that is all we really have.

Living your life looking forward enables dreams to stay alive.

Being Happy Always Begins With Being Grateful!

The Dalai Lama was once asked why the poorest of the poor, living with mud floors and having nothing, can smile and be happy, while the rich often seem miserable. The Dalai Lama laughed and said, of course! What was obvious to him is not obvious to us. He explained that many of us who have much, live in search of acquiring the next thing, and then the next thing, and so on. Those individuals live in a constant state of want.

The Dalai Lama explained the poorest of the poor are often happy if they are protected from the elements and have some food in their stomach. They live with gratitude for the simple things of life. Those with much have forgotten or never knew what it feels like to have nothing. Accordingly, they are not grateful when their morning breakfast is plentiful, available, and mostly excellent. Instead, they will think that their coffee was not the right temperature, their eggs could have been less runny, or their toast had the wrong butter or jam on it. Those with few possessions are happy with a bowl of food, a cover over their head, and a blanket to keep them warm.

While it is natural to strive for nice things, the pursuit of such things does not have to consume us. When we live in a state of want, we have compromised happy. Much of this mind set has been planted in our brain from outside influences. We live in a culture which stresses competition pitting us in a fictional competition with our friends, neighbors, and loved ones. When we adopt this mind set, we are never satisfied unless we are ahead of the next person. And since we will always be behind in some way, or will not have something, or will not have become something, we will always be living in a state of lack.

This is more than an ordinary disease in our society of much, it is an epidemic. So many of us are unhappy that we have not gotten what we believe we deserve. I am not Implying that you should not work hard and strive for nice things. What is important, is appreciating the nice things you have or have earned. It is all right to strive for new things. It is not all right to be so consumed by the desire for the next best thing. That mindset will cause you to ignore the wonderful things you already have.

It has often been stated that we should live with gratitude. To express gratitude is to get up in the morning and be grateful for running water, a warm home, good health, and the good health of our loved ones. It is to be thankful for food, a good job, nice clothes, and a car that gets us to work and home at night. If your destination is happiness, the road that you must be on is called Gratitude. If you are always on the road called Want, that is exactly where you will find yourself at the end of your journey. If you live with want, you will always want!

Move to Gratitude Lane, it is where you want to live.

Most Folks Are About as Happy as They Make Up Their Minds to Be

Abraham Lincoln said this many years ago. Happiness is not about what happens to us, as much as it is about how we handle it. Life presents all of us with tough times. The question is how will we handle it? A mind that returns to gratefulness is certain to shorten the period of difficulty and build a road back to happy.

It has been said an optimist sees a glass half full; a pessimist sees a glass half empty. An optimist sees a kinder, gentler world that will return to goodness.

Happiness is a state of being. It is advisable to create a system within your brain to find your way back to happy. You do that by liking yourself and being excited about the days to come.

Choose happy!

At Any Given Moment of Life

There Are Millions of Things You Can Be Thinking About

Happy People Focus on Positive Things

Life is what you focus on. By the time you receive your high school diploma from your principal, you understand life can be tough. That's just the way it is. But life is also wonderful. It is important to understand you have a right to enjoy your life.

Teach yourself to smell the roses, to relish the laughter, to bathe in the love given and received. Dedicate yourself to exploring, learning, and experiencing. Most importantly, find the greatness in doing for others.

Life is a collection of moments and the ones you focus on shape your life. Whenever possible, focus on joyful thoughts. It is the better way to go.

Happy people focus on positive things.

The Brain Evolves With Time and Experience

No one teaches us that the brain changes as we age. To better explain, let's think about a fictitious party. In the middle of the party two 15-year-olds get into a fistfight over a foolish argument. Luckily it is broken up by friends and no one gets hurt. The party goers may think of the two combatants as foolish and immature, but they will quickly move past it. Now let's change the scene a bit at our fictitious party. Two 37-year-old guests get into a fistfight over a foolish issue. As with our two teenagers the fight is broken up, no one gets hurt, and the party goes on. Except every party goer is disturbed at the behavior of the two men. In fact, remarks such as, "I've never seen anything like that," become a common part of the party conversation.

Obviously, there is a difference in what took place in the two separate fights. The difference is the age of the combatants: teenagers in one case, individuals in their late 30s on the other. But what is the real difference? Why are we shocked more by the behavior of the adults than the teenagers? Of course, the behavior of the adults was a complete surprise, hardly ever seen in respectable company. And the teenagers? Foolish, regrettable, immature, but not unheard of. In fact, fights among teenagers at parties can be common when alcohol is present. But alcohol is present when people in their late 30s get together, yet fistfights among that age group are unexpected and very unlikely to occur. So, what's the difference? The brain…

When we are teenagers and adults, we make decisions with two portions of our brain: the amygdala and the pre-frontal cortex. So, what's the difference? The number of decisions made by the amygdala is proportionally higher in the teenage brain. The amygdala is our fight or flight button. It senses danger and it reacts. It does not process past events because it doesn't store past events. These are compiled in the pre-frontal cortex. We know through modern-day brain research that teenagers often use the amygdala for crucial decisions. As we age, however, we rely on the stored information in the pre-frontal cortex to determine the right decision.

Years ago, a movie was made in which a group of boys lay down in the middle of the road as traffic passed by them on both sides. It was meant as a test of bravery.

Unfortunately, a few boys who saw the movie, went out and copied the behavior. The amygdala decided it was all right to copy a foolish stunt in a movie. The boys lay down in the middle of the road and one was run over by a car and paralyzed. As we grow older, the accumulated knowledge in our pre-frontal cortex would have told us the foolishness and dangerousness of such an act.

The important thing to know is that alcohol, peer pressure, and other teenage experiences frequently influence the amygdala to make our decisions for us. Once you understand your brain, you will understand it is best to step back, take a breath, and ask the pre-frontal cortex for a decision.

Our brain is an evolving decision-maker.

Create the Rules of Your Life So You Win

As we leave high school, so many of us don't recognize we have already set up a scoring system in which we lose over and over. Life is a game in which we are involved in creating the rules for how we live. Surprisingly, many of us set up the *Game of Life* so we can't win. Many of us desire to be better, improve, and take our performance to the highest level we are capable of. Many of us make lofty goals and work to achieve them. This is especially true if we are capable, gifted, or born with advantages.

As we achieve goals, we promptly replace them with the next level of goals. We rarely pause for more than a moment and celebrate the achievement. We have not been taught how to step back and reflect on how hard we worked or how well we applied our talent. Our society has planted two subliminal messages into our culture that has set us up to be unhappy. The first, if we have met our goal or goals, they were probably set too low. And the second, once you have achieved a goal, stopping to reflect on the achievement will result in future failure based on a lack of motivation. Simply put, too many of us set up the *Game of Life* so we lose.

Also, when we reach a goal, we are trained to raise the level of expectation often without appreciation of what we have achieved. If you are an athlete and make All-Conference, you should have been All-County. If you are All-County, you should have been All-State. If you are All-State, you should have been All-American. If you are Salesman of the Month, you should be the Salesman of the Year. If you are Salesman of the Year, you should be Salesman of the Year every year. If you achieved that, you should have owned the company. On and on until we lose at the *Game of Life*.

In my case, I was once named the County Teacher of the Year. A wise colleague approached me in the hall and said: "Congratulations!" I responded, "well, I don't even know if I am the 4th or 5th best teacher in my department." The colleague looked at me and said, next time just say thank you. Over the years, I have often reflected on that encounter. I had an exceedingly difficult time admitting that I was good at what I was doing. I learned a lesson that day from an older and wiser colleague. I began to realize that I continually set up the *Game of Life* so I would lose. By doing so, I was sure I would drive myself harder and not accept a lesser effort.

Of course, in my mind I thought this thinking pattern would drive me and I'd be more and more successful and that would make me happy. The problem with that thought pattern was it was all based on a cultural lie. When we set up the *Game of Life* with rules that never let us win, we are compromising our happiness.

Set up the Game of Life so you win!

A Positive Temperament Is a Hidden Superpower

Long before leaving high school, you probably have heard the phrase, "someone has an attitude." Having an attitude is another way of saying a bad disposition. Life variables such as wisdom, intelligence, and talent are often thought of as the keys to success. Often overlooked is one of the most important ingredients in success and happiness: temperament.

When I coach someone who is going to a job interview, I teach them the first rule they must understand. The person who gets the job is the person the employer would like to see walk in the door Monday morning. That person is invariably the one with the best disposition. A person who is easy-going, competent, pleasant, easy to smile, concerned with others, and even-keeled, is likely to get the job.

Famed Supreme Court Justice Oliver Wendell Holmes at 92 years old was visited by Franklin D. Roosevelt (FDR). After Roosevelt left, Holmes reminded those present that he was appointed to the Court by FDR's cousin Theodore Roosevelt. He then said, "...a second-class intellect, but a first-class temperament." Which Roosevelt he was speaking of was unclear. Although vastly different men, both Franklin and Theodore had first-class temperaments. Both had overcome tremendous health issues but still were able to attack life with vigor and a smile. A positive temperament is key in all relationships and job situations, but it is most welcome in leaders. Having a positive temperament gives you a marked advantage in winning the *Game of Life*. You will have success in your relationships, and you will be better equipped to handle the tougher moments of life.

A positive temperament leads to a successful life.

With Many Life Choices

A "Do Over" Is Always on the Table

When you are asked about what you will do with your life after high school, you will likely choose college, military, or work. People will expect you to have the answer when you may still be trying to figure it out. What others may not understand, is you are making life decisions a few years removed from being a middle schooler. Most importantly, when you graduate high school, you do not have a large experiential base to understand what each option may offer. You are being forced to choose a path when you have not explored what life has to offer.

Much thought goes into which college a high school senior will attend. However, decisions are made with insufficient information. Until one is living at or attending a college, they are making their best guess as to whether it is the right fit. It might help to think that choosing a college is a short-term commitment. If it turns out to not be the right fit, a transfer is not particularly difficult.

As we move on in life, it is best to read, listen, explore, and consider as much as possible. A friend of mine on his 26th birthday, told me he was confused regarding what to do next. He had graduated college and worked a couple of worthwhile jobs, but none were really for him. He chose to go to the library and do research. For the next six months he explored careers and created a new path forward. Based on his research he made new choices and became very successful. He had gained knowledge and used this new information to consider his options. The choices we made yesterday may not be the right ones for today and tomorrow.

Always remember, it is never too late to stop, reconsider, and change paths.

There Are Few Things in Life as Powerful as a Great Mentor

Having a great mentor is an extraordinary gift. If on your travels you come across a person who has great wisdom, insight, and cares about you; work to make them your mentor. A mentor can often make the difference between good choices and bad, right decisions and wrong, the correct road and the wrong road.

Many have heard of Carnegie Hall. It is named after Andrew Carnegie. He was the premier steel producer of his time. The super successful Andrew Carnegie started his business life as a mentee. Thomas A. Scott took in Carnegie as a young boy and mentored him. Scott took extra time to explain to Carnegie why he was making each decision. The result of Scott's mentoring was that Carnegie grew up to become the richest person in the world. Luckily, Carnegie learned and prospered at the hands of an older, wiser man who cared about him and worked on bringing out Carnegie's best qualities.

Keep your eyes open and hopefully a great mentor will come your way. And if you find one, hold on, the ride will be worth it. You may not become the richest person in the world, but you will most certainly be enriched.

A great mentor is a hidden treasure.

Always Plan for Tomorrow

But Always Live for Today

Life is a paradox. This means we must consider two very different scenarios for every crucial life decision we make. We must consider how life decisions affect today and tomorrow. This is especially relevant as we graduate high school and college.

It has been said sarcastically that a college freshman wants to save the world; a junior wants to make a living with a meaningful career; a senior just needs a job. It is important to understand we have many life transitions. Each time you reach a pivotal moment in life, take a breath, assess where you are, and realize that life is a journey.

With each new journey, it is best to start at the beginning. Don't be afraid to get more training. Don't be afraid to work for less money as you gain experience. Although the immediate problems of life will always direct us to think about today, it is important to consider the long-term positive and negative consequences.

We all gain much by focusing on the bigger concepts of life. Sometimes this balancing act between what is good for us today, but important for us tomorrow, can be quite difficult. If you consider both, you have a better chance of making the right decision based on the information you have. That is the best we can do for no one knows what tomorrow will bring.

Always consider tomorrow but live for today.

Academic Debt Can Lead to Regret

I was asked by a local college to hold a 3-day seminar for first-generation college students. Each student was the first in their family to attend college. I spent considerable time planning on how best to advise them on maneuvering through the matrix of college life. When I asked them what they really wanted to know, I was surprised by the overwhelming question of whether college was worth the financial commitment. I was surprised because the students were attending a state university and some of them may have been getting financial aid. However, debt is a real issue for students who come from limited resources.

For many students, including the middle class, there are seductive offers of student loans. Many students run up huge, back-breaking debt that will be gladly offered by lending institutions.

My advice on this is simple: a little debt may be the cost of doing business. Heavy debt should never be undertaken without a real plan of what it will mean for your future.

Be careful, today's dream loan may become tomorrow's nightmare.

Life Is Not a Sprint

It Is a Marathon

Life is not a sprint or a quick race to see who wins. Life is a marathon. The person on top at 25 may be the one looking back with regret at 75. Despite popular wisdom, there is no age at which you should have achieved anything.

Moving forward each day at a deliberate pace is a recipe for success. Many of the most successful people struggle throughout their 20s only to find themselves and their success a little further down the road.

The most important thing is to stay optimistic if success does not arrive quickly. After the first season on network television, *Cheers* and *Seinfeld* were among the lowest-rated shows on television. Still some network executives believed in them and left them on the air. They subsequently became two of the most successful shows in television history. Tom Brady had to share time as the starting quarterback in college. He was then drafted in the 6th round. Today he is widely considered the GOAT (greatest of all time).

Success comes in its own time, not ours.

The Right Answer May Not Be in Your Answer Box

Too often we look for answers to problems in our answer box. Unfortunately, with the tough issues of life, the answer may not be there. It is fair to say, the road to success is shaped by the times we live in. Each generation has a different shot at success. Some graduate at a time with a booming economy. Others graduate at a time of economic difficulty. If you are graduating during a bad economic downturn, it is especially important to think out of the box. Answers for your success may not come from concepts you presently have. Thus, the practice of thinking outside your box of answers (things you presently know) is often crucial to success.

Thinking out of the box can make all the difference between success and failure. The Russians had a multi-year lead on the United States in the race to the moon. Today we know they lost. But what was the problem that the Russians could not solve that the American engineers did? Both the United States and Russia had the same problem to solve. The United States was able to find answers from outside the box, Russia wasn't. The problem? How does one spaceship leave Earth's orbit, journey to the moon, land on the moon, and then return to Earth? The technology of the middle 20th century simply couldn't solve the problem.

The engineers needed to look out of the answer box because the answer wasn't there. United States engineers searched for answers and designed a spaceship with modules that came apart. One module gave the ship the thrust to leave earth's orbit, another module carried the astronauts to the moon and back to earth, and a different module landed them on the moon and then returned them to the main ship. As a result, the U.S. landed men on the moon and Russia never did.

These scientists were able to find answers outside of the traditional answer box. They were engineers who could have been our neighbors. They looked for solutions outside of the answer box and found a method for landing astronauts on the moon and successfully returning them to earth.

If people like us and our neighbors can solve such a complicated puzzle, it serves as encouragement we can find the answers we are looking for as well.

Keep looking, the answer you seek may not be in your answer box.

Sometimes You Have to Go with Your Best Guess

My dear friends had an elderly Uncle Bob who once upon a time was an important person in engineering. That was the extent of what I knew about him. Soft spoken and nice, that may have been the end of it. But one holiday dinner we were talking, and the conversation revealed something in Uncle Bob's career. It turned out that Uncle Bob oversaw the team that tested the Lunar Excursion Module (LEM). The LEM which was to land men on the moon and get them back to the main ship.

In life you never know who you are talking to and what you can learn from their life experiences. Uncle Bob was the one that NASA and Head of Flight, Gene Krantz, called after the explosion on Apollo 13. The question to him was, could the LEM support life in space to get the astronauts home? As it turned out, the main ship lost so much oxygen, the astronauts had to abandon it and use the LEM as a rescue vehicle. Bob answered, "I need six months of testing to give you an answer." They told him he only had six minutes. Uncle Bob's answer: "In my professional opinion, I think so." He was right! Sometimes in life you just have to go with your best guess. I think so, worked!

Life experiences help you make the best guess when answers are not clear.

To a Fish the Lake Is the World

A fish in a lake can only see the water and what is in it. There is no world outside the lake. How many of us can only see our immediate world? How often do we not see what others are seeing?

We all live in our own head, which means that we see the world through our own paradigms and perceptions. We tend to think others think as we think. And if they don't, we think they should. The more we can get out of our own head and think as others think, the higher our emotional quotient rises. Emotional quotient (EQ) is the ability to understand how others feel and relate to them based on that understanding. A strong EQ helps provide the ability to be socially successful, well liked, and a good friend.

Learn to listen and consider what others are saying. A perfect day is different for each of us. To think that everyone wants the same things you do, indicates a need to explore the thoughts of others.

If we better understand the world that another person comes from, we can better understand their pain and motivation. It can help us develop empathy for those we meet on our journey. Empathy requires understanding. Understanding requires the ability to put yourself in the shoes of another and see the world through their eyes.

Try to see the world as others see it.

The Value of Money Is Based on What You Do With It

The most important value of money is not to have a bigger boat or better car. The most important value of money is it can be used to make many problems go away. On a bad day your refrigerator may break, or your air conditioning may stop cooling, or your car won't start. If a problem arises and money will make the problem go away, and you have money, you do not really have a problem. Money is there to make problems go away.

It is also true that money can provide the ability to experience the things that bring us joy. For some it will be a tropical vacation, for others it may be a vintage car; we all want different things. We can also use money to buy back free time. Extra money allows us to pay someone to do the chores of life that otherwise would fall to us. Money allows us to be philanthropic and help others.

Money can provide a sense of freedom. Freedom from fear of not having enough. Freedom to allow us to explore other options in life if we are not happy with the ones we presently have.

Money also helps us provide options for those we love. Improving the lives of those we love, brings us joy.

It is important to remember that having and making money is not an end. It is best used to solve problems, help others, and enjoy some of the things that life has to offer.

The value of money is what you do with It.

Live Today

So You Don't Regret

When Today Becomes Yesterday

Time is the currency of life. How do you spend your currency? Time is a funny thing. When we are 18, each year is 1/18 of our life. When we are 50, each year is 1/50 of our life, a much smaller chunk. As we age, in comparison to our entire life, each year seems to fly by quicker.

What we learn later in life is the importance of how we spend our time. It is important to plan but as we plan for the future, it is crucial that we do not sacrifice the present. So many of us put off today's happiness for the promise of a happier future.

When people look back, they discover that a balanced life would have yielded much more happiness in the end. The Romans used the phrase, Carpe Diem. Translated it means, seize the day.

Hospice nurses dealing with people at the end of their life, report that one of the greatest regrets people have as they move on to heaven is how they spent their time. Invariably they realize too late that they should have spent more time with family and less time with work.

Time and the choices we make about how we spend our time, is a huge portion of how we evaluate our own lives as we knock on heaven's gate. We all will run short of time at the end.

Live today in a way you don't regret today, because today will become yesterday.

The Real Hero Makes Lives Better

Our heroes at 18 are frequently not our heroes at 40. As humans we need role models; people who have come to represent what we aspire to be. We also live in a world of celebrity and super wealth. Too often we choose heroes from the world of the talented, the wealthy, the successful. We do that because it is common sense to want to follow in the footsteps of those who have achieved what we would like to achieve. We seldom look at their values, their lives, and how they conduct themselves.

Growing up in the 50s and 60s I shared my hero, "The Mick," with millions of other fans. He could run faster, hit farther, and the media portrayed him as the All-American boy from Oklahoma. However, Mickey Mantle was plagued by personal issues that turned a nice, decent person into someone quite different; especially when he was drunk. Some of my other heroes included rock stars, entertainers, and politicians with a polished image but who were deeply flawed.

In June 2000, I was a day away from leading the graduation class of Long Beach High School into their commencement exercises. I had written my obligatory principal's graduation address when it became apparent that I had more meaningful things to say than what I had written. My thoughts were on two unlikely heroes of mine from the Class of 2000. Unlikely, because they were my students. Justin had died of cancer. When he was well enough to come to school, he would turn down rides from school personnel, saying that he could do the walk. I visited him at home when he got sicker and was amazed by his courage. His best friend was Dennis who was confined to a wheelchair because of Spina Bifida. Dennis did not want pity; he would adapt to his circumstances the best he could and then move on. Dennis and Justin were my heroes. They had courage in the face of harsh and difficult circumstances. They did not engage in self-pity.

Heroes should not just be the gifted and talented who are exercising their God-given talent. Heroes should be those who overcome, endure, give-back; do the little things for a community or a person to make lives better. We are surrounded by heroes. They are the moms and dads who go to work to take care of a family. They stay up at night to take care of a sick child. They help neighbors in times of need.

The heroes are the police, firefighters, teachers, and sanitation workers who go the extra mile for others. Heroes are those with courage and empathy who turn their thoughts into positive actions. Heroes are those who show us who we could be and what we could do during our journey through life.

At the end of his life "The Mick" said no one should consider him a hero. He told people to never emulate the type of behavior he displayed throughout his life. He wanted others to be better. At the end, Mick finally became a real hero by helping others as he championed and encouraged organ donations.

Heroes are the special people who make the lives of others better.

Life Was Never Designed to Be Fair

Life is not designed to be fair. I wish it weren't so, but it is. One of the things that becomes evident to principals who are keen enough to recognize it; students use fairness as an evaluative tool. Did they see the punishment coming for an action or was it a surprise? Are they being treated fairly? Did their teacher grade more harshly than their friends' teacher? The questions around fairness permeate student life. It is not just student life; we all judge life based on fairness.

We often ask ourselves if we got a fair deal in life. Were we emotionally harmed by insufficient or cruel parenting? Were we born with physical or mental gifts? Did we have the resources to go to colleges that would give us the best opportunity for success? Did we find ourselves at a young age in a battlefield surrounded by pain? Life presents each of us with different challenges. We all have different lessons to learn and as such, different experiences, and thus different lives.

It's not fair that one child comes from a home with an alcoholic parent and the other comes from a home where the parent is loving, kind, and mentally healthy. It is not fair that one person is born with Spina Bifida and his best friend in high school dies of cancer. It is not fair that sometimes the good die young and those who are hurtful seem to go through life with little accountability. Life is not fair. But here is what we missed. Life was not designed to be fair.

All lives have a wall in front of them. On one side of the wall is unhappiness. We have a choice when we come upon this wall. We can yell at fate for what has befallen us. Or we can work the problem and figure out how to get to the other side of the wall. On the other side is happiness and a quality life.

The dirty secret is the wall is a different height for everyone. Some are born with a wall so low that a person can take an easy step and they are over it and into an easier life. Others are born with a wall so high it seems impossible to scale and successfully get over. Here is the deal; no one will hold a pity party if your wall is 20 feet high. If you dwell on unfairness, you will never get over the wall.

Regardless of the size of your wall, start building a ladder with optimism, conviction, and courage to meet the challenge. Dennis with Spina Bifida got over the wall. He is happily married, works in the medical field, and enjoys life. And there is no free ride for the person who has the incredibly low wall.

Challenges find everyone in life. No one goes through life unscathed. Some are born with everything and turn it into nothing. Some are born with nothing and turn it into everything. We have the power to turn our lives into a meaningful and quality experience. But it starts with finding a way over our own personal wall.

In the end it is not what your challenge was, it is what you did with it.

Always Lead With Kindness

It Will Open Hearts and Doors

As you graduate, the coming years will bring many changes. This advice is for tomorrow, because soon today will be tomorrow. One of the challenges for many of us will be dealing with young people.

In the world of education, I have often heard, "I am teaching them responsibility." Too often, that is a catch phrase for arbitrary regulations and harsh treatment of young people. There are a multitude of ways we learn responsibility in life. If we don't learn it, we pay a steep price. Life will make a young person learn one way or another. I have never seen a study that said if you are mean while you are teaching responsibility to a young person that the young person will benefit from it.

Often adults can be blind to the methods they use to teach responsibility. One year a group of students came to see me because their English teacher had assigned a rigorous project over the Christmas break. While I agreed with the students, they deserved a vacation and quality time with their families, I informed them their teacher had every right to make the assignment and they needed to complete it. They countered by telling me she did the same thing over the shorter Thanksgiving break and never graded it. When she gave the students this assignment, they asked her if she would mark their Thanksgiving projects over the Christmas break and return them in the new year. She responded, "I'm not working over my vacation." The moral of the story is don't ask others to do something you wouldn't do.

I believe in leading with love while teaching young people to be responsible. I used a phrase in my schools to reflect this, "high expectations, high support." Without support, the expectations are just mean. When dealing with young people, lead with kindness. There will be times when you must be tough and hold them to appropriate standards. Two things must be done in these cases. First, be clear as to what the consequence will be if the young person does not do what they need to do. Second, be sure you live to the same standard that you expect from others.

Many positive outcomes result from kindness and understanding.

We Don't Get Over Loss

But We Can Learn to Live With It

Sometimes life will punch you in the stomach so hard you can't catch your breath. Every life has downturns; some lives are much more difficult than others. For those suffering, they are often told by friends, family, and therapists, with time you will get over it. That is simply not true. We never get over the great losses of our life. Painful loss is an outgrowth of wonderful love. The best we can do during these times is to strive to move forward. But get over it? That is not going to happen.

There are moments in almost everyone's life that are incredibly painful. We wonder how we can get through the pain of those times. It is important to mourn, and it is important to grieve. After a loss, there will always be a missing piece where your heart and love reside. There will come a time when it is important to move forward and begin to heal.

President Biden puts it eloquently when he says that one day a smile will come to your face before a tear to your eye, when you think of a lost loved one. People mean well when they tell us one day, we will get over it. But with effort and time we do learn to live with loss and pain and find our smile again. Those who have passed on to the other side would want that for us.

The loved one you have lost would want you to find your smile once again.

During the Tough Times We Need Others

Wouldn't it be great if we could look into the future? As we graduate high school, we have little evidence of how each of our classmates' lives will turn out, as well as our own. We can make educated guesses based on the approach each classmate takes, but we still don't know. For most, there is a little magic and a little tragic, just as Jimmy Buffet says.

The ability to deal with the difficult times of life will test your ability to be resilient. Those who love you, hope you can bounce back into life, and enjoy the good moments to come.

At times, that can be difficult. If you do not find yourself successfully moving on after a difficult situation, seek help. During tough times, we need each other the most. Sometimes a professional therapist is best equipped to help us reflect and find a path back to happiness. Whether it is a friend, a loved one, or a therapist, remember during the tough times we need others.

As we proceed through life, we need others to sustain us through our journey.

There Is a Time Limit to Sharing Your Pain

People will support you emotionally for a period of time when life does not go your way. With tragedy or loss, the support of friends, neighbors, and colleagues will likely be there for you. They will offer support, love, and understanding until they need to move on. Then they expect you to get over it, or else you will go from being a sympathetic figure to someone they want to avoid. It's just the way it is.

At one point in life, my wife and I experienced a terrible loss. It was summertime and I was the assistant principal of G.W. Hewlett High School. As I walked down a long hallway, a group of people saw me and promptly ran up the closest staircase, rather than come face to face with me and my tragedy. They were good people, just unable to deal with my pain. That happens…

Friends and family who are strong and can handle our difficult times will be there with us. But many good people will get overwhelmed by our difficulties and move to protect themselves from our pain.

Forgive others who don't understand your pain; they are often doing the best they can.

We Are All One

The original *Star Trek* had an episode in which there were only two survivors of an entire planet. The two survivors were at war with each other over skin color. The crew of the Enterprise was perplexed as each man had a two-color face: one side completely white, the other side completely black. The crew pointed out to one of the survivors, you look the same. And to the crew they did look the same. Exasperated by this perceived oversight, one of the planet survivors explained that the right side of his face is white, and the right side of the face of his enemy is black. A fact that meant nothing to anyone other than the two survivors of the planet. When the two last inhabitants left the starship and returned to the planet, they proceeded to end all human life based on their hate.

It is important to ask yourself if you categorize people in your mind based on race, religion, or color. Can we be hiding something from ourselves? It might be interesting to look inside to explore our hidden perceptions of people based on race, religion, and color.

As we proceed through life, understanding how others deal with the world and how we deal with the world is an important skill to acquire. The more we get to know people of other cultures, the more we realize they want the same things for themselves and their children. We may be from different cultures, but we are all one.

Regardless of the divisions we have created, we are all one.

College Graduation Is About "Sticking to It" Not Intelligence

As you leave your high school graduation ceremony, you will be thinking about your next stage of life. For many it is entering the world of higher learning. College is a different world. There is no one looking over you. It will seem they don't care if you don't show up for class. It will seem they don't care if you are struggling. Except they do care, and they can provide support systems if you seek them out.

If you went to a big high school, you might have been less likely to find support. However, even in a big high school you were more likely to have a caring teacher watch over you than on a college campus. You need to know there is a world of support on college campuses, but you must look for it. If you need to find academic support; it is there. If you need counseling; it is there.

Above all else, you must drag your tired butt to class even when you don't feel like it. Even if professors do not ask where you have been when you miss class, because most likely they won't, you still need to go. If you are struggling with a course, you must seek academic support and not fall behind.

Intelligence will make college easier. However, you must be a mature advocate for yourself on a college campus, even if you don't feel up to being a mature advocate. Perhaps the most important lessons of college are to learn how to advocate for yourself and to work through problems.

The ability to be resilient and stick to the task at hand will lead to success.

Only Special Friends Are Truly Happy for Your Success

Funny thing about many people; they want to go back to old workplaces, reunions, or just run into people they once knew and regale them with tales of success. Often, they don't realize those stories make others feel less successful or worse yet, that their life is less meaningful. This situation can very likely result in others cheering for the person to fall on their face. The Germans call it Schadenfreude: the act of being happy because of another's misfortunes.

Of course, there are friends who may try to bask in the success of others success by virtue of knowing them. That is a lot better than the crowd cheering for the person to fall from grace, but still not ideal.

But if you are fortunate enough to find a friend who is genuinely happy for your success, without benefiting in any way from it, you have found a unique, secure, special person. Hold on to them tightly, they are special.

Remember to be gracious about your success.

Your Best Friend on Graduation Day May Play a Very Small Part in Your Life Tomorrow

It is hard to grasp at this moment in time, but your best friend may not even be in your life in the near future. Many relationships are situational and based on a "time in the life." Those of us who have the same best friends throughout our lifetime are lucky. For the overwhelming percentage of us, people come and go throughout our lives.

One of the reasons Facebook has become so successful is because it helped us find friends from yesterday. Because of this contact we can catch up and sometimes enjoy remembering days gone by. Then we move on because relationships are situational, and the old friend is not part of our lives today. The people you work with at a job, hang out with in high school, meet on a sports team, room with at college, are for the most part, passing through your life at a time and place.

Many of our relationships are situational. It is best to consider choices we make considering this "time and place" friendship or relationship. When a person is trying to pressure you into doing something you are not comfortable with, they may just be passing through your life. However, the life decision you make, based on their encouragement, could last a lifetime. So be careful about peer pressure when your instincts are telling you to choose differently.

The advice of today's best friend may be tomorrow's regret.

Is Your Influencer Good for You?

Chris Gardner whose life was portrayed through the movie *Pursuit of Happiness* said that in high school Pookie was his buddy. Of course, as his buddy, Pookie had some influence on him. But Chris decided that Pookie's influence would not determine the course of his life.

We are all independent thinkers. At the same time, we are also influenced by others. When we were children, our parents were in our inner circle of influence. During our early life, we may also have in our inner circle siblings and babysitters. As we grow older and enter the school years our inner circle of influence gets more crowded with new friends. When we become a teenager and communication might be strained with authority figures, our parents may have found themselves moved out of the inner circle. The friends we have at the time almost always have an enormous impact on the decisions we make. The irony is these friends are likely just passing through our lives in a particular time and place.

As the years pass, we move into the various stages of adulthood. The influence of our parents during these years is largely determined by the type of relationship that has been built over time. Our new influencers may come from neighbors, co-workers, our spouse, and more.

It is important to note, today's media world has manipulated and influenced us by using logarithms to analyze our patterns of thinking. Media then feeds us more of what we already think. As a result, we become caught in an echo chamber of only hearing and seeing what we already believe. Often, we are sure we see both sides of an issue when the reality is, we do not. To retain our ability to think independently requires our diligence in evaluating who is influencing us. We also must consider if the influencer is really acting in our best interest. This is crucial throughout our lifetime and perhaps never more important than during high school and college years when so many life decisions are required.

Chris Gardner grew up to be a financial success in life and the movie was made to illustrate the path he chose. Chris Gardner didn't let Pookie decide his life path.

You shouldn't let your Pookie determine your life path either!

The Perception of Others Becomes Their Reality

Many years after high school graduation, the G. W. Hewlett High School newspaper hunted down graduates and asked them about the piece of advice they received in high school they still remember and use. A wonderful young lady spoke about advice I gave her when I inquired about the fight she was having with another student leader. She responded by telling me that they were good friends and they were only kidding. Without much thought I blurted out it is critical to remember that perception becomes reality in the minds of others.

We live in a world in which the image others have of us, negative or positive, becomes their reality. This perception can come into play regarding important issues. The former student told the newspaper that she always remembers that in life, perception becomes reality for people. That is still as true today, as when I first told her that many years ago.

To others, you are what they think you are.

If You Think Computers Do Not Make Mistakes, You Are Making a Mistake

Working on this book, I wrote the phrase "she responded." The spell check corrected a comma to a semicolon. Then it recorrected itself back to a comma. And then back to a semicolon and then back to a comma. It is a software feature on a computer. Computers are growing in their ability to think but they also make mistakes. With the onset of artificial intelligence, the mistakes computers make can be scary come tomorrow and have long term disastrous effects.

As graduates, many of you will be in important positions affecting others. Please remember that computers and artificial intelligence are capable of mistakes. Those mistakes may not be as innocent as the difference between a comma and a semicolon.

Be wary of artificial intelligence!

Communication Is a Tricky Thing

Warning: Emails and Text Messages Are Often Misinterpreted

My son who is a talented writer has a t-shirt that says, "Commas Save Lives." The t-shirt expresses the point this way: "Let's eat, Grandma vs. Let's eat Grandma." The comma after eat, implies dinner is ready. Without the comma, the implication is that Grandma is dinner. Appropriately, the caption on the t-shirt says, "Commas Save Lives."

We communicate in many ways. It has been said that in a one-to-one conversation, actual words are only 7% of a message. Voice inflection, distance between the people interacting, facial expressions, hand movements, and more, provide information when communicating. All these message clarifiers are not present when we text and email. A word to the wise: carefully read each text and email for how the other person may interpret or misinterpret your meaning. Additionally, try to refrain from bashing or speaking poorly of a person in writing. It is never a good idea. The negative things you say in writing may come back to haunt you one day.

The most important piece of advice regarding emails, in life and the workplace: **never** hit by mistake, Reply All. By doing so you just shared your thoughts with everyone. If there is a negative comment or opinion, by virtue of Reply All, you have shared it with the group. Ouch!

And remember, never forget the comma for grandma's sake. :)

What in the World Is Cognitive Dissonance?

The human brain is a marvel, a wonder, and yet it is curious. The brain when it has a firm opinion on an issue doesn't accept conflicting information. For example, a person who considers himself a good person, yet does the wrong thing, invariably finds a way to justify the action. Therefore, their positive self-view remains intact. When some in society create derogatory terms for a group of people, they are justifying the wrong in their own mind by assigning a hurtful name to the group. By creating this false persona for the other group, the brain can harbor prejudice and still feel it is following moral goodness. This is cognitive dissonance.

I experienced cognitive dissonance with a department leader who didn't care for my authority as principal. I met with her to try to bridge the gap and improve our relationship. In the discussion she accused me of never thanking her for the things she did in the school. I corrected her and said I thanked you in person and in writing. She corrected me and said I have never thanked her once. I walked over to my desk and pulled out a copy of a thank you letter I had sent her two weeks earlier. I placed the letter in front of her. She looked at it and said to me "like I've said, you've only thanked me once." Cognitive dissonance! She didn't want to work with me and was going to find a way regardless of the facts. I could have shown her other thank you letters I sent her, but that would have been an exercise in futility.

Cognitive dissonance allows us to maintain the self-concept we are a good person even when we do bad things. As a result, bad actions become more frequent and systematic within a society.

People live in the world their mind creates, whether it is true or not.

We Never Recognize These Are the Good Old Days

While We Are Living Them

As humans we look to the future for more money, time, peace of mind, etc. As we focus on the future, we are likely missing that today may be quite special. One day you may look back fondly on high school friends and times of innocence. You may appreciate all the wonderful times you had growing up with your family. You may love your young body that was healthy and vibrant when you were 18. Unfortunately, too often we don't enjoy the time while we are living it. We often do not recognize these are the good old days, while we are living them.

In the movie *City Slickers*, three best friends go on a challenging excursion, each in search of meaning as they approach their 40th birthday. The character played by Billy Crystal finds meaning in the wisdom of an old dying cowboy. The old cowboy tells him the meaning of life is one thing. When asked what the one thing is, the cowboy says that's what you have to figure out. The one thing is different for everyone. But I suspect for most, the meaning is found in family and love.

Use your time for the people and things that are really important because these are the good old days. For many of us, we often romanticize the past. When we do that, we tend to remember the things we are fond of and forget yesterday's struggles. If you are healthy and your family is well, if you have enough money to put food on the table, a nice roof over your head, and you have meaningful work, these are the good old days.

As the Romans said, Carpe Diem, Seize the Day!

A Broken Soul Hurts Other People

When a child is emotionally hurt, they often become insecure and damaged adults. Sometimes the insecure turnaround and do major damage to others. They become energy thieves, robbing others of their energy through their cruelty and creation of fear.

It is important to know that souls can be fixed. I worked with a very fine person who told me she had lost her mother when she was young, but her father remarried a wonderful person who took care of her and made her feel warm and loved.

Boys and girls who are hurt badly by life when they are young, may do grave damage to others as the years pass. However, the damage can be mitigated if there is an intervening variable of love and support. In fact, love and support can help almost every soul.

Love and support can heal the soul.

That New Acquaintance May Not Be What They Seem

Sociopaths have the ability to be extremely charming and charismatic. They have a broken soul. Some broken souls are more broken than others. When an individual is greatly damaged, their soul has receded to a dangerous level. Their soul has disconnected from the universal good. The sociopath is such a person. These individuals are often able to hide their toxic behavior behind a winning personality.

These individuals have been greatly damaged, usually in childhood. Often they experience great emotional trauma, or they have been raised by unbalanced people. As a result, they spread damage. They lack the ability to develop empathy for others who are in pain. They also need attention and power to feed their damaged soul.

Adolf Hitler was a typical sociopath: charismatic, damaged, heartless, vicious, self-serving, self-righteous with an undying belief in his own infallibility. The sociopath seeks power and influence over others as a means of self-gratification.

The sociopath also has the ability to charm and convince others because they find it easier to lie than tell the truth. Sociopaths have unique and identifiable characteristics. They also leave a wake of damage in their path. Look for the warning signs because sociopaths come off especially charming when it suits their needs. So, if you meet someone who is unusually charming, charismatic, and in a position of power or seeking power, it doesn't mean they are a sociopath. However, it does mean you are best served to watch them carefully. Ask yourself if they are untruthful, narcissistic, and easily capable of cruelty.

People are often blind to the truth right in front of them.

Never Rob a Person of Their Dignity

If you want to get a negative reaction from a person, and you don't have a great deal of time, disrespect them. For sure, disrespect compromises a person's dignity. If you take away their dignity by disrespecting their ability, looks, decency, importance, or relevance; you will create a mortal enemy.

One of the most important ways a leader can gain support is by showing respect to those with less authority or power. Feeling respected is one of the most important things human beings need to live in balance.

Take away the dignity of another, and it is often worse than a physical injury.

Don't Flaunt When You Are Right

It Only Serves as Proof You Are Insecure

It is great to be right. But if another person is wrong, your being right does not mean you win. It means you are correct on the issue but can still lose the encounter. Learn to correct with grace and class.

If you are a boss, how you correct others will be a large part of how you are viewed. It is always best to advise others with kindness, especially when dealing with children. If you must prove you are right, you are also proving you are not very secure.

Flaunting your advantage over others will not serve you well in the long run.

Arrogance Is Not Cool

A cousin of obnoxiousness is arrogance. When we are good at something, really good, arrogance can often be a by-product. It is easy to behave in this manner when something comes easily to us that is hard for others. This behavior is unbecoming and quite unbearable for others and curtails self-reflection. When we live in this state of mind, we always think we know what's right. The truth is no one always knows. We are all wrong from time to time.

Arrogance is not endearing us to others. If we are arrogant, others do not step in to help us avoid foolish mistakes. Arrogant people are not warned of potential mistakes for several reasons. Others believe they would not except the good advice anyway. Additionally, others would like the arrogant to fail. As stated earlier, the German word Schadenfreude means others are happy for our misfortune.

Arrogance grows Schadenfreude, just as water and sun grow flowers in the spring.

Addiction Overrules the "Know Better" Brain

As previously stated, we make the best choice we can with the information we have at the time. Except that is not always true. This concept is not true for addicts who know better and make the wrong choice because of their addiction. An alcoholic may know it is wrong to take that drink, but at the time, the condition did not allow for another choice. The alcoholic is powerless over the addiction at the time. The same is true for all addictions. Sometimes things are simply unsolvable without help from others. Sometimes we need an intervention.

If you find yourself in this type of situation; shame, regret, self-anger, and self-pledges of future better behavior, are all useless. The addict needs to find the strength to acknowledge their reality, forgive themselves, and seek effective outside help. Friends and loved ones need to say to the person, we love you, and that is why we are intervening. We are holding a mirror up for you to see what your life has become and what your loved ones think is best. Friends and loved ones often find the addiction is still the boss until some variable gets the addict to acknowledge that a different life course is necessary for survival.

It takes a lot of courage to confront an addict and the failure rate of confrontation is extraordinarily high. The addict won't seek help until they decide to. But friends still need to try to help in the way they consider best.

Addiction steals the will to do the right thing.

Drug Use Is Russian Roulette

If someone takes a six-chamber revolver and puts one bullet in it, spins the chamber so they don't know where the bullet is, they are all set for a game of Russian Roulette. Russian Roulette is a game of chance with a potential tragic outcome. It is taking a dangerous and stupid risk. It is an idiotic enterprise to engage in.

There are several reasons that people take drugs and drink alcohol. People take unprescribed drugs and drink to an excess because of social pressure, the desire to feel better, and to gain the acceptance of their chosen group. As people embark on this behavior, they invariably have a belief they can avoid long term problems despite their behavior. Sometimes they are right. Sometimes they are wrong.

The thing about drugs and alcohol is that some can walk away from it and some cannot. Countless lives are ruined by drugs and alcohol. More lives are lost to addiction than can be easily counted. It is never very wise to play Russian Roulette with your life. Taking a drug is like putting a revolver to your head with some bullets and some empty chambers. When you pull the trigger, you never know if the chamber is loaded or unloaded. You never know if you will be the one to walk away or the one who will have their life taken from them. At first, virtually everyone thinks they are the one who will be able to walk away. Of course, that is not true. Drug usage is inherently a dumb thing to do. Case closed.

I can't remember anyone ever telling me that drugs or alcohol improved their life.

The Short Distance Between 18 and 65

There is so much that is great about being 18. Your whole world is in front of you. At some point we are all 18 years old. Those of us who look at those years in the rearview mirror know that in many ways we are not the same people we were at our high school graduation. We have different motivations, concerns, and things that make us happy. We regret the times we were unkind and the years we wasted.

Once upon a time, high school principals in my county had an end of the year retreat to reflect, talk, and strategize. We invited guest speakers and learned from them. One year, we had an older administrator who was retiring and reflecting on his life and career. He spoke to us about the loss of time with his family and the choice he made to work rather than be home. It appeared to have ruined more than one marriage. At 18 we rarely consider that we must balance career success with family time for a better life.

We must always consider that meaningful employment is a key to our self-respect. Living in balance will often leave us with tough choices about how we use our time. It will be a personal choice with each situation. But whenever and wherever possible, remember in the end, it will be your family that was the most important part of your life.

It is a short distance between 18 and 65.

People Want Change

Except They Often Don't Want Change

The perplexing thing about people and change is they want it until it occurs. As people we don't like what we don't like. We complain about it, sometimes without end. We want change! We hate a status quo that leaves the things we don't like in place. But what virtually no one will tell you is there is something people often have more problems with than the status quo: change that shifts the ground beneath our feet.

Change is scary and leaves people off balance. The status quo is familiar and unchallenging. We want change, but do we really? Are we comfortable living in a new reality, even if it is one we have created? If you are in charge and you think if you make change that is requested by the group, that all will be fine, think again. People are used to what they are used to. Change can be upsetting, except people don't realize it until the change is enacted.

Pleasing people is a perplexing art form.

Much of the Bad Is Temporary

Bad may be replaced by good because in many cases, bad is temporary. Many of the bad things presently in our life will pass with time. So, enjoy the good times. Smile often and laugh with gusto. And when times are bad, just remember the bad times will often pass.

The quickest way to get the bad times to pass is to attract positive outcomes through positive thoughts. Think positive thoughts and they become a radio antenna to the universe to send you good stuff.

When going through the bad times of life, remember the good is right around the corner.

Cults Beyond Reason

There are many good things about belonging to a group. Those with strong family ties and strong bonds of friendship can count themselves among the lucky. However, our need to belong can also lead to recruitment into cult-like groups. These groups may advertise themselves as mainstream religious or political advocates. But often they are fringe groups seeking to control and manipulate. Cults are artificially formed groups which at the beginning attract people with a seductive message. The attraction is in the belonging.

When dogs are in a pack, they act differently than they would on their own. A calm dog can become vicious. The dog pack is an analogy to what a cult does to people. Once again, the major attraction of the cult is in the belonging. Once you are in a cult, you belong to something larger than yourself. However, the cult culture can lead to brainwashing and manipulation of purpose.

Throughout history there have been political cults. Hitler formed one in Germany in the 1930s, and others have followed his model. His model was to tell you who to fear, who to blame, and who to persecute based on their differences. This cult model has been copied numerous times.

Once a member of a cult, people will do extraordinary things that are quite out of character; things they would have never done on their own. Just like a peaceful dog will do when in a pack.

Be wary of groups that try to recruit people during the college years. Groups can be motivated by good or bad. If the cult is trying to manipulate you to think only what they think, do only what they do, follow only what they tell you; you know which type of group you have found.

Even when you are part of a group, always maintain your moral compass.

The "Other" Is A Weapon

There are numerous individuals and groups who want control over people. The most common trick of those who seek control is to create a group to demonize. The group they target is the "other." Those who ruthlessly seek power utilize fear of the "other" as a political tool. The "other" is the group used as a scapegoat for numerous problems. As a consequence, the "other" becomes a target of ridicule, condemnation, and often violence.

The targeted group is always labeled with a nasty, offensive, and demeaning nickname. The purpose of the nasty identifier is to dehumanize the members of this group. It is much easier to hurt people if they are thought of as deserving mistreatment.

Hate is an ugly thing. To get good people to hate the "other," fear of the "other" is introduced. They are told that the "other" has hurt and will hurt you and your family, your country, and the things you love. This technique allows them to have power over you and your thoughts. The "other" is merely a tool in their arsenal to gain control.

It is hard to hate the "other" if you know them and their families. In this life you can either embrace love or hate. It is wise to steer clear of those who peddle hate and fear as vehicles for control. Because ultimately, they want to control you and persecution of the "other" is simply their vehicle to achieve that goal.

In this life you can either spread love or hate. Choose love.

The Driving Forces of Life

There are two main emotions that drive our decision-making process: love and fear. When we make healthy decisions, they often come from love. When we make unhealthy decisions, they often come from fear. The more decisions we can make with love, the better our lives will turn out.

Tony Robbins articulates that we have two main fears: not having enough and not being enough. The more you know who you are, and like who you are, the better you can deal with those two fears. Love is the antidote to fear.

In life it always comes down to love.

Empathy and Balance

Good people are empathetic by nature. It is important to be empathetic. We understand others by thinking of what they must be going through and how to help them on their path through life. But there is a cautionary tale to be learned about empathy. Feel too deeply, care too much, feel pain too extensively, and you will find yourself in a state of burn out. The most committed and those who feel the most are often the people who burn out first. As a result, people in that group will be much less able to be there for others.

When I was 17, I worked in a camp for kids with cerebral palsy. One boy named Lee, took a real liking to me and was always happy when we came in contact. He was in a wheelchair and I just assumed he had cerebral palsy. It turned out that Lee had muscular dystrophy and was declining at a fast pace. I took it so hard that I had no desire to return to that camp in subsequent years.

I took that lesson into my classroom and the buildings I supervised. I was always empathetic to those in need. But I learned to protect myself by understanding that there is a lot of pain in the world. The best way I could help others is by feeling for them but not pitying them. I accepted this was their fate and the best I could do is be there for them, but also protect myself so I could be there for the next person in need. I would not run away when a student lost a parent, instead I embraced them and helped if I could.

I learned if a person is in pain, I can't help them if I jump down into the hole with them. I needed to stay out of the hole and throw them a lifeline. My job was to help ease people's pain, not be consumed by it.

By understanding empathy, we can be there for people in need.

The Elusive Truth

When I grew up there were three major TV stations. The country got its news from one of the three reputable sources. The TV news did not target liberal or conservative audiences. The news media of yesterday attempted to be politically neutral to attract viewers from a general audience. Today's media is motivated by profit rather than by serving the public good. As such, media is built around a niche market; people who believe the same concepts. Of course, it feeds us more of what we already believe. To the media companies, the truth is less important than making money.

We used to battle in the United States about ideas and philosophies. Today we battle about what is truth. Today, the liars are often the first ones to accuse the other side of lying. Hitler did it in Germany in the 1930s. He called the press "Lugenpresse," which translates to the "lying press." Hitler, the sociopath, was a masterful liar. But there are many who lie, manipulate, and prosper in our world, aided by a social media which does not feature a moral compass.

There are alternative ideas and concepts and we should always consider the thoughts of others. But a fact is a fact, alternative facts are creations by those who want to manipulate us.

To be informed in today's society one must search out truth.

Depression and Us

Sometimes life can be so tough depression can be an outcome. There is no shame in being depressed. If you find yourself in a state of depression, it is wise to seek help. It is hard to solve depression on our own because the decision maker we use to solve problems is in the same place the problems live. Depression lives in the brain. The solutions to solve depression also must be instituted through the brain.

Getting past depression can be a tough fight! But if you are depressed it is important to note that you are not at fault. You have done nothing wrong, and you need to forgive yourself for not being able to overcome it on your own.

Try better food, exercise, walks in nature, a good therapist, and if needed, appropriate medication. But don't think depression is your fault. It is part of the human condition. Depression can be overcome. Always remember that problems are most likely temporary, even if we don't realize it at the time.

Depression is a temporary condition.

If we cannot find a way back to happiness on our own, help is available.

Bad Feelings Reappear

Anger, regret, past problems we believe we have overcome, return when we are in a receptive state of mind. A movie, comment, song, smell, or a variety of things can bring back a bad memory. That is important to know. Anger for example, must be put back in its rightful place before it starts to fester inside. Bad thoughts have a way of living within our bodies like a virus that is hiding. When something creates a negative thought, it can serve as a stimulus sparking the return of bad feelings. It is normal and something that can happen to virtually all of us.

It is best to understand that bad feelings may reoccur. As a result, it is important to develop a thought process which will allow us to circumvent the negative thoughts. There is nothing gained by dwelling on bad feelings. In fact, it does significant harm. The easiest way out of this hole is to think about something that brings you joy and gratitude.

Bringing in the light is the best recipe for getting past the dark.

Don't Be a Professional Victim

Unfair things will happen to you. I know this because unfair things happen to all of us. At one time or another we are all victims of mistreatment from others. The important thing is to never become a professional victim. Professional victims expect bad things to happen to them. They expect people to be unfair and try to take advantage.

If you approach life that way, you will draw negative energy to you. The message you are sending to the universe is negative and will constantly reinforce that you are a victim. When you say to the universe that bad things are always happening to me, picture the universe as the *Genie in the Bottle*. The response from the *Genie*: your wish is my command.

Instead, picture yourself as someone who has learned from a bad experience and therefore won't have to experience that again. Negative thoughts attract negative events in our lives.

Always remember that positive attracts positive.

Know Your Talents and Limitations

We have many sayings in our society that are simply not true. One of them is you can be whatever you want to be. Just work hard at it. The correct statement should have been, you can be whatever your talent and skill set allow you to be. Just work hard at it. We all have different talents and skill sets; pursuing success in the areas we have talent is a winning philosophy.

One of the important qualities to have, is the ability to evaluate what you are good at, and what you are not good at. There are numerous people who are talented and quite successful in their field. Sometimes a person is successful in a multitude of areas.

But success in one area is not a guarantee of success in another. In fact, there are many sports owners who were successful businessmen who have not been able to translate their skill set in business into successful sports ownership.

The lesson is: if a person is great in one area, or lucky at one thing, there is no guarantee that it will translate to other businesses or pursuits in life. Understanding this will help you make smart decisions about what you pursue in life. If you can do that, your chances of success are greatly enhanced.

It is important to recognize what you are good at and where you need help.

All the World's Problems

One of the things we all know from a young age is there are problems in the world. There are problems in the world when we are born and there will be problems in the world throughout our lives. New problems replace old problems. Old problems never seem to go away.

As a teenager, I thought once the United States got out of the Viet Nam War, life would be pretty good for the many. But the end of the Vietnam War did not solve world hunger, disease, sociopathic leaders, cruelty, injustice, racism, etc.

Many of us who try to make the world a better place are following our soul's true purpose. This is the University of Life, a place to learn and grow. Success is in the effort to make the world better.

The true importance in life is the effort we make to help others during our time on earth. Our success is helping others breathe a little easier. We may not solve the problem, but if our efforts help others even a little, we have achieved success and the experience helps our soul grow.

When it comes to the world's problems, we should just do our best.

Leave Every Place You Go a Little Better

It is important to have a philosophy of life. A philosophy of life acts as a compass to ensure that you are on the right road. My philosophy of life is to always try to leave a place a little better than I found it. Can you imagine how great our world would be if everyone made each place we pass through a little better for us having been there? If there is a theme for a successful life, I would recommend it is just that. If you are looking for a philosophy of life, feel free to use this one.

Make every place you pass through a little better because you were there.

Patience Really Is a Virtue

A lack of patience will often cause us to make decisions which in the long run are the wrong choices. Switching jobs prematurely, looking for immediate gratification, not working through a problem; can all be by-products of a lack of patience. We all want what we want, now!

There has been research on children who cannot delay their reward. They would prefer one piece of candy now, rather than wait and get two pieces later. Research reveals children who cannot wait for the reward are more likely to be less successful.

Patience is a virtue. Often in real life, the tortoise does beat the hare. People tend to measure success in the short run. Real success can only be determined with the passing of time.

Having patience will also let you slow down and enjoy the wonderful moments of life. Slowing down and enjoying the ride that life gives us takes practice.

But here is the deal. There are great moments of life. It is important to know them when we see them. Enjoy them, revel in them. Treasure them! They are special and part of the gift of life. But if we lack patience, are always lost in our mind, are always on to the next task quickly; we will miss the best parts of life.

Practice patience, enjoy life, success comes in its own time.

Carpe Diem

Seize the Day

There are many great philosophies on the best way to live. One of my favorites comes from Winnie the Pooh. This is not an exact quote, but it encompasses the main concept: <u>Today is my new favorite best day!</u>

I suggest saying that each morning. I just wonder if it would get your day off to a good start.

It will certainly encourage you to enjoy some honey with your breakfast 😊.

Make the best of every day.

History Teaches Us to Never Give Up

History is filled with stories of people whose best days came after they thought all was lost. There was a man who lost his mother and his wife within hours of each other. He was left with an infant daughter to raise. He went on to become the Police Commissioner of New York City, the Governor of New York, and the President of the United States.

Be strong and be resilient. Better days can be just around the corner. Just like they were for Teddy Roosevelt.

The most successful people are those who never give up.

Live In the Right State of Mind

An extraordinary percentage of people live a life with compromised happiness. Obviously, it is easier to be happy if many things go right. But even that is no sure guarantee of happiness. But happiness is also something we can positively influence by having the right state of mind.

Live with gratitude, choose happiness, replace bad thoughts with good thoughts, and like yourself.

God does the best work and you are his creation. So, what does that say about you?

Train yourself to live with a happy frame of mind.

The Secret to Happiness

Almost seven decades of research has helped me discover the "Secret to Happiness." It was there all along for us to discover but like the things we pass everyday but never see, we pass the "Secret" without realizing it. The "Secret to Happiness" is not money, celebrity, artistic achievement; although all those things can be nice. The "Secret to Happiness" is genuinely liking ourselves.

How do we come to like ourselves? It is always in terms of how we treat others. We always define ourselves in terms of others. There is a simple test you can perform to prove this. Ask someone if they are a nice person? They will most likely say yes, or I try to be. Then ask them, how do you know you are a nice person? And they will always define it in the following way: I know that I am a nice person because I am always kind and never try to hurt anyone. Or I am a nice person because I'm there for others, or because I am good to my family, or I treat others the way I want to be treated.

When we are selfish we live in a contradictory manner to our own happiness, without ever realizing it. People who like themselves find meaningful things to do with their time. They find their joy in making life better for others. Simply stated, we find the "Secret to Happiness" in the face of others.

Helping others is truly its own reward.

Spiritual Theory in High School

High Schools never touch on spiritual theory. They never discuss the root of evil, reincarnation, or the soul. When physics teachers create curriculum, they rarely delve into the mysterious concept of energy.

This section is based on questions regarding the universe. Please explore and do your own research. Due to politics, high schools can't engage in these types of discussions. But spiritual topics may be of interest to you in your lifelong pursuit of knowledge.

The Mystery of the Quantum Universe

In the physics classes I observed as principal, I never witnessed a discussion of why Einstein was in search of a single theory of the universe. In the 1920s, electron microscopes were invented with the ability to see quantum particles. The quantum world is invisible to us with the naked eye and traditional microscopes. It is simply too small for us to see.

When the quantum world was first seen, the observations shocked physicists. This amazement was shared by the most famous physicist of all time, Albert Einstein. What they discovered was particles in the quantum universe do not operate under the same laws of physics as the universe we observe. In the visible (or larger) universe, there is a cause and effect for movement. For example, in the universe we understand, H_2O molecules will vibrate faster or slower based on temperature. At low temperature the molecules vibrate slowly and become ice, at a middle temperature they vibrate faster and become water, and with enough heat, the H_2O molecules vibrate so fast they turn to gas.

In the quantum universe the movement of particles does not seem to follow a pattern. They just do what they do. Physicists cannot explain why particles in the quantum universe move without explainable cause or effect. There has been much speculation as to why that happens and what it means. The early theories speculated that the quantum universe operates under chance: no law of physics. Einstein completely rejected that theory and made a famous statement that has often been quoted but seldom understood. He said God is not playing dice with the universe. He meant quantum particles which appear to move under a different set of laws are not operating by chance. Something is happening and just because we can't explain it does not constitute chance. Einstein spent the rest of his life trying to figure out what was happening in the quantum world. He was never able to. Maybe one day, one of you will.

To summarize, the particles on the quantum level and the visible world operate under two unexplainable different principles of the universe. That has awesome meaning, unfortunately the meaning is still above our ability to understand…at this time!

There are great mysteries of the universe that still need to be solved.

Something Created Us

I personally believe there is overwhelming evidence there is a God. Anyone who thinks we just evolved from minerals and dust tends to believe only what they can see. Therefore, in their world everything must be explainable and/or visible. If we follow their reasoning, there is no air or water vapor, or viruses transmitted through the air. Because we can't see them.

The simple fact is our creator exists in a dimension we cannot understand in human context. As a result, some decide there is no creator. But for the rest of us, our relationship with our creator becomes of paramount importance.

There is tremendous evidence there is a creator and everything we do during our stay on Earth has importance to the universe. The one overriding theme that follows the concept of a single creator is what is wanted of us during our stay on Earth. I believe the answer is very clear. Be good, be kind, and be caring for each other.

This may be a concept you may wish to explore in greater detail.

There is a creator who wants us to be kind.

Everything is Energy

If you looked at your hand under an electron microscope you would see particles moving. We are energy that has slowed down in vibration to exist in a solid form. As discussed, depending on vibration, H_2O exists as ice, water, or water vapor.

Water vapor vibrates more quickly than water and water vibrates more quickly than ice.

The fact that we are energy which has slowed down into a physical form is a clue into the greater universe.

The concept of energy is hard to describe. But energy powers our homes and us.

Without energy there is no life. Is life therefore energy?

Energy Flows Where Attention Goes

Energy thieves steal your energy. Have you ever been around someone who thrived on making the lives of others terrible? Or had a relative who when they showed up, brought misery with them? These broken souls are energy thieves. After dealing with them, we are physically and emotionally wiped out. They create conditions in which you think about them, curse them, fear them, and always want to be rid of them.

All the while, they are stealing your energy as a fuel for their survival. They never stop stealing energy because they never actually realize they are not getting what they need. What they really need is love and kindness. However, they can't get that because they are misguided in their pain and they spread pain wherever they go.

Regardless of their issues, you still suffer when dealing with an energy thief. Energy grows within us through kindness, forgiveness, helpfulness, selflessness, and unconditional love. These are all qualities an energy thief does not recognize because they have been damaged on the soul level: usually early in life.

In Dickens, *A Christmas Carol,* Scrooge is an energy thief who does damage to all he encounters. Three ghosts enlightened Scrooge about the damage he was doing. If the energy thieves in our lives were visited by three ghosts, we'd all breathe easier.

Damaged souls work to steal the energy of healthy souls.

The Medium and the Brain Scientist

Do mediums really communicate with the dead? On an episode of Dr. Oz, he arranged for Dr. Daniel Amen the brain expert, to conduct an extensive examination of the Long Island Medium, Theresa Caputo. It was a novel idea by the producers and was a fascinating segment.

After Dr. Oz did the introduction, Dr. Amen came on camera with Ms. Caputo and announced that he had tested her brain waves while she was in a mental state of contacting the dead. Dr. Amen announced that the brain waves were virtually still as if in a state of hibernation. He reported he had only seen it once before in his research and that person also claimed to be able to communicate with the dead.

Dr. Amen also stated that while backstage with Ms. Caputo she began to communicate personal information to him from loved ones on the other side. Information that Dr. Amen confirmed was both true and virtually impossible for Ms. Caputo to know.

Dr. Daniel Amen, brain expert, stated he was totally convinced that Ms. Caputo was able to communicate with the dead.

Our loved ones may truly be watching from the other side.

The Findings of a University Study of Mediums

About two decades ago, a scientist at the University of Arizona did a comprehensive experiment on five of the top mediums in the world. The scientist recruited individuals who were to be the subject of the medium sessions. The mediums never met the subjects before and knew nothing of them or their lives. To make it more difficult, the medium and the subject were separated for many of the readings by a sheet to prohibit the ability of the medium to read body language.

The scientists created a mathematical measure to quantify the results. Following the experiment which featured five mediums, the scientists concluded that the mediums had over a 90% accuracy rate. This meant the overwhelming amount of information that the medium stated about the person was accurate.

Interestingly, the mediums identified a deceased pet dog entering the room for one of the subjects. It is a fascinating concept to think our favorite dog is waiting for us on the other side.

More research would be a welcome addition to our understanding of life and death.

Memories of Another Life

Many decades ago, Professor Ian Stevenson, Chair of Psychiatry at the University of Virginia, began an on-going research project of children born with the memory of a prior lifetime. The University of Virginia has over 2,500 cases they have documented of children who credibly spoke about a life before their present life. The details provided by the children were frequently beyond any rational explanation, other than the children seemed to have memories of a prior life.

Do we come back from life to a new life to learn new lessons?

The Strange World of
Synchronicity

The universe operates with concepts that we frequently don't understand. One of those concepts is synchronicity. Synchronicity is when things happen beyond a reasonable chance. But they did in fact happen. For example, in 1996 the Yankees honored Yogi Berra by dedicating a day to him. Because he was a catcher, they thought it would be fun to have him catch the first ball, rather than throw it. So, they chose Don Larsen, the only pitcher to throw a World Series perfect game (caught by Berra) to throw the first pitch to Berra. Berra didn't have a catcher's glove so the Yankee catcher, Joe Girardi lent him his. Larsen threw the ball, Berra caught it, and gave Girardi back the glove. The regularly scheduled game then got underway.

David Cone, who was pitching for the Yankees, then proceeded to throw a perfect game. Girardi caught the perfect game with the glove Berra had worn a little over two hours earlier. Don Larsen who threw the first perfect game in Yankee history looked on as

Cone pitched the third perfect game in Yankee history. A year earlier David Wells threw the second perfect game in Yankee history. It just so happened Don Larsen who rarely attended Yankee games was also in the park that day. These types of coincidences are examples of synchronicity. When things happen by unusual chance, it can make us wonder what the universe was up to. If this story wasn't enough synchronicity, David Wells and Don Larsen both graduated from the same high school in San Diego.

Synchronicity is when things happen beyond a reasonable chance.

Karma

I believe there is Karma and there is heaven. Karma is the universal score card for doing right or wrong things to others. If I am correct, leaving every place you go a little better is not only the right thing to do, but it also brings good fortune to you.

Be good, be kind, be empathetic. It is the right thing to do.

Graduation from high school takes place at your school's Commencement Ceremony.

Commencement is a beginning not an end.

What is commencing is the next stage of your life!

When you are confused or lost and in search of meaning,

Love is the answer.

<u>Love is the most powerful force in the Universe.</u>

Now that you have graduated, have a great life, and make the world a better place because you came this way!

About the author:

Dr. Richard Gary Shear is an award-winning educator and a national consultant on school reform to universities, school districts, and educational organizations. He has created and advised on numerous programs that focus on topics in education: the teenage brain, school safety, at-risk students, environments for success, and initiatives to improve the lives of students and educators. Schools utilizing Dr. Shear's recommendations have experienced unprecedented growth in student achievement and graduation rates, enhanced self-esteem among students, and improved school safety. Dr. Shear can be contacted at: http://linkedin.com/in/richard-shear-5781509

Made in United States
North Haven, CT
03 April 2023

34955306R00070